MOVING OUT ON YOUR OWN

Emily Hutchinson

SADDLEBACK
EDUCATIONAL PUBLISHING

MAR

21st CENTURY

LIFESKILLS

Moving Out on Your Own
Everyday Household Tasks
Health and Safety
Managing Money
Consumer Spending
Job Search
Getting Ahead at Work
Community Resources
Transportation and Travel
Car and Driver

SADDLEBACK
EDUCATIONAL PUBLISHING
www.sdlback.com

ISBN-13: 978-1-61651-123-4
ISBN-10: 1-61651-123-0
eBook: 978-1-60291-854-2

Printed in the United States of America
15 14 13 12 11   1 2 3 4 5

CONTENTS

PREVIEW | Readiness for Independence

■ How much do you already know about the material in this unit? Circle words or letters to correctly complete the sentences. Answers are upside down at the bottom of the page.

1. To live on your own, you must develop (independence from / dependence on) your parents.

2. Competent adults are able to solve (everyday / elaborate) problems.

3. A person with positive rather than negative attitudes about challenges in their life is (more / less) likely to be successful.

4. The first step in changing a bad attitude is to (deny / recognize) that it is a problem.

5. Most efficient adults use (a calendar / their memories) to keep track of appointments.

6. A daily "to-do" list can help you (avoid unpleasant jobs / budget your time).

7. What is one item you might put on a daily to-do list?
   a. get out of bed
   b. take a shower
   c. see dentist at 11:00 A.M.

8. The main part of most people's income is from
   a. a job.
   b. a trust fund.
   c. a savings account.

9. To avoid debt, you need an income that is at least equal to your
   a. rent.
   b. expenses.
   c. taxes.

10. What is not an essential skill for living on your own?
   a. filling out forms.
   b. driving a forklift.
   c. understanding directions.

Answers: 1. independence from 2. everyday 3. more 4. recognize 5. a calendar 6. budget your time 7. c 8. a 9. b 10. b

LESSON

1   Knowledge and Skills Checklist

Most young people are eager to become independent adults. What does it take to make it on your own in today's world? One way to judge your readiness is to inventory your competencies. What's the current level of your knowledge and skills? What additional knowledge do you need? What basic skills require more development? This lesson can help you identify how far you've come—and how far you need to go—along the path to successful adulthood.

GENERAL SKILLS: Next to each essential skill, rate your achievement level from 1 to 5. Be honest!

STRONG				WEAK
1	**2**	**3**	**4**	**5**

I've developed the ability to . . .

1. _____ balance my wants and needs.

2. _____ work hard for what I want.

3. _____ manage my money.

4. _____ express myself clearly.

5. _____ make wise decisions.

6. _____ resist peer pressure.

7. _____ respond to emergencies.

8. _____ cooperate with others.

9. _____ manage my time.

10. _____ solve everyday problems.

SPECIFIC SKILLS: Show your competencies by writing **Y** for *yes* or **N** for *no.*

I know how to . . .

1. _____ take care of my health.

2. _____ cook simple dishes.

3. _____ write a résumé.

4. _____ manage a checking account.

5. _____ dress appropriately for different occasions.

6. _____ investigate job opportunities.

7. _____ use the library and Internet to find information.

8. _____ prepare for a job interview.

9. _____ make and stick to a budget.

10. _____ schedule an appointment.

11. _____ make simple home repairs.

12. _____ use public transportation.

13. _____ write a business letter.

14. _____ fill out forms properly.

15. _____ get information from maps, charts, and graphs.

16. _____ get legal help.

17. _____ understand and follow directions.

18. _____ take care of my clothes.

19. _____ apply for a driver's license.

20. _____ register to vote.

■ **Thinking It Over:** Check the correct sentence endings.

A competent adult can . . .

1. ____ use basic tools.

2. ____ plan a healthy diet.

3. ____ pay cash for everything.

4. ____ balance a checkbook.

5. ____ read a bus schedule.

6. ____ avoid serious illnesses.

7. ____ save as well as spend.

8. ____ make and keep appointments.

■ **Synonyms and Antonyms**

1. What word in the lesson is a synonym (same meaning) of *preparedness*?

   _____

2. What word in the lesson is an antonym (opposite meaning) of *foolish*?

   _____

Write **S** for *synonyms* or **A** for *antonyms* next to each word pair.

3. ____ essential / necessary

4. ____ specific / general

5. ____ require / need

6. ____ succeed / fail

7. ____ eager / reluctant

■ **Everyday Math**

1. The best score on the General Skills survey is (high / low).

2. Suppose you rated yourself a 3 on each General Skills competency. Your *total* score on that section would be (30 / 50).

■ **Giving Examples**

1. Tell about a time you *responded to an emergency*.

   _____

   _____

   _____

2. Tell about a time you *resisted peer pressure*.

   _____

   _____

   _____

3. Name three simple dishes you know how to cook.

   _____

   _____

   _____

4. What might you wear for a job interview?

   _____

   _____

   _____

■ **On Your Own**

Name an important adult skill that's not mentioned in the lesson.

_____

_____

LESSON

2 Attitudes Assessment

Suppose you've acquired the necessary knowledge and skills to go out on your own. Good for you! Now it's time to check out your attitudes. What are your basic ideas and beliefs about yourself, others, and the world around you? Do they tend to be negative or positive? Good attitudes can help you through many difficulties and make your life much happier. Bad attitudes can create serious problems and make you miserable.

Do you realize how negative attitudes reveal themselves in your behavior? Read the following examples.

ATTITUDE	BEHAVIOR
"I'm always right."	• blames others for one's own mistakes • resents constructive criticism
"I'm no good if I'm not perfect."	• makes excuses • avoids responsibility
"Might makes right."	• loud and pushy • won't compromise
"Rules are meant to be broken."	• disrespectful of authority • tardy; argumentative
"The world owes me a living."	• lazy and slow-moving • expects something for nothing
"Why try? Things never work out for me."	• sets low standard of achievement • readily accepts defeat

No human being is perfect. To one degree or another, all of us tend to have some harmful thinking habits. How do *you* express your negative thoughts and feelings? Be honest with yourself. When you're under pressure, do you tend to be a know-it-all, a bully, or a victim? Are you a perfectionist or a hothead? Are you deliberately slow or even defiant about following directions? Do you give up too easily because you *expect* to fail? These are only a few of the negative attitudes that limit success.

Of course it's easier to see bad attitudes in others than it is in ourselves. Think, for example, about someone who gossips all the time. Trying to make yourself look good by making others look bad is a sign of insecurity. The gossiper may not realize that—but other people do. They know they can't trust a person who gets attention by calling attention to other people's problems.

Success in life begins with making a good impression on others. So it only makes sense to check out your attitudes. Some of them may be immature or downright self-defeating. If so, you've already won half the battle just by recognizing them! Changing attitudes takes time, patience, and lots of practice. But the good news is that you *can* do it if you really want to.

■ **Thinking It Over:** Write **P** for *positive* or **N** for *negative* next to each attitude statement.

1. ____ I try to be grateful for constructive criticism.

2. ____ Other people seem to get all the lucky breaks.

3. ____ Asking for help makes me look dumb and weak.

4. ____ I often feel like everyone's out to get me.

5. ____ I take responsibility for my own mistakes.

6. ____ I see many opportunities when I watch out for them.

■ **Synonyms:** Draw a line to connect words with the same meaning.

1. behavior   a. correct
2. beliefs   b. errors
3. defeat   c. accomplishment
4. achievement   d. actions
5. mistakes   e. thoughts
6. right   f. failure

■ **Inference:** Cross out the *incorrect* sentence endings.

1. Other people can often recognize your attitudes in your

   body posture.   facial expression.
   eye color.   tone of voice.

2. Confident people tend to be

   cheerful.   enthusiastic.
   moody.   cooperative.

■ **Key Vocabulary:** Complete the sentences with words from the reading.

1. Constructive *c*_____ is the act of pointing out errors and suggesting ways to improve.

2. An *i*_____ person doesn't feel safe or confident.

3. Each side gives up something when a disagreement is settled by *c*_____.

4. An *a*_____ is a way of acting that shows what one is thinking or feeling.

5. An *i*_____ attitude is childish or foolish.

6. To be *t*_____ is to be late for work or school.

■ **On Your Own**

1. Name two of your own *positive* attitudes.

   _____

   _____

2. Name two ways that negative attitudes could hurt you in the workplace.

   _____

   _____

   _____

   _____

LESSON

3 Budgeting Time

Have you learned to organize your time? All successful adults are good "time managers." They schedule their activities to make sure they won't fall behind. They remember important dates because they plan ahead.

Jessica has a hectic schedule. She goes to school every weekday, and she works a part-time job. From time to time, she has appointments. And she has regular chores to do in the apartment she shares with her roommates. In addition to all this, she has a social life. How does she keep her schedule straight? How can she remember where she has to be at any given time? Jessica has a system for budgeting her time. She keeps track of what she needs to do by entering it on a calendar that's on her cell phone, so she can look at it throughout the day. Here is her calendar for September:

Sunday	Monday	Tuesday	Wednesday	Thursday	Friday	Saturday
		1 class 8-12 work 1-4 study 4:30	2 class 10-2 work 4-6 gym 6:30	3 class 8-12 work 1-4	4 class 10-2 work 4-6 gym 6:30	5 chores 9-11 Sanjay 7:30
6 study	7 class 10-2 work 4-6 gym 6:30	8 class 8-12 work 1-4	9 class 10-2 work 4-6 gym 6:30	10 class 8-12 work 1-4	11 class 10-2 work 4-6 gym 6:30	12 chores 9-11 family bbq 3:00
13 study	14 class 10-2 work 4-6 gym 6:30	15 class 8-12 work 1-4 study 4:30	16 class 10-2 work 4-6 gym 6:30	17 class 8-12 work 1-4 haircut 4:30	18 class 10-2 work 4-6 gym 6:30	19 chores 9-11 Mia's wedding 7:30
20 study	21 class 10-2 work 4-6 gym 6:30	22 class 8-12 work 1-4 Alex's bday	23 class 10-2 work 4-6 gym 6:30	24 class 8-12 work 1-4 Dr. B 4:30	25 class 10-2 work 4-6 gym 6:30	26 chores 9-11 Sanjay 3:30
27 study	28 class 10-2 work 4-6 gym 6:30	29 class 8-12 work 1-4 library 4:30	30 class 10-2 work 4-6 gym 6:30			

Jessica also creates a daily to-do list on her phone. Every evening, she looks at her calendar. Then she makes a list of things she needs to take care of the next day. She lists only those tasks that are special for that day. She does not include everyday routines, such as brushing her teeth or getting dressed. She goes over her to-do list throughout the day. Then she either checks off or deletes each item as she does it. Here is her to-do list for September 16:

- English homework 8–9
- math homework 9–9:30
- classes 10–2
- card—Alex's birthday
- gift—Mia's wedding
- work 4–6
- gym 6:30

10

■ **Thinking It Over:** Write *yes* or *no* next to each sentence.

1. ____ You should put information about your next dentist appointment on your calendar.

2. ____ Every day, you should put "brush teeth" on your to-do list.

3. ____ Put your friend's birthday on your calendar so you won't forget it.

4. ____ A calendar is a good place to keep track of a changing work schedule.

5. ____ A daily to-do list should include long-term goals, such as "Buy a house."

■ **Everyday Math**

1. Noah worked 4 hours a day, 5 days a week, at his part-time job. How many hours did he work in 4 weeks? _____ hours

2. On Tuesday, Sofia worked 5 hours, attended classes 4 hours, and spent 1 hour getting back and forth. She also spent 3 hours doing homework. How much time does she have left for sleeping, showering, dressing, eating, exercising, and chores? _____ hours

■ **Key Vocabulary:** Circle the word that best completes the sentence.

1. A *hectic* day is (busy / easy).

2. An *appointment* is a (surprise / scheduled) meeting.

3. A *chore* is a (routine / complicated) task.

4. Another word for *system* is (list / method).

5. To *include* means to (keep in / keep out).

■ **Cause and Effect**

1. The reason you should put appointments on a calendar is

   _____

   _____ .

2. A to-do list is helpful because

   _____

   _____ .

■ **On Your Own**

Write your own to-do list for tomorrow.

_____

_____

_____

_____

_____

_____

11

LESSON

4   Budgeting Money

Living on your own forces you to manage your money carefully. That means making a spending plan. Follow these steps to establish a basic budget.

1. **Figure out what your income is.** Consider all sources, such as your job, gifts, allowances, and student loans. Base your job income on your actual paycheck, not your salary. Remember that part of your earnings will be withheld for taxes.

2. **Decide what you can afford to spend each month.** How much can you afford to pay for rent? How much should you spend on food? What about transportation, utilities, Internet, and phone costs? You'll also need to budget for insurance, health care, clothing, and a certain amount for entertainment. What percentage of your income should you spend on each? Here's a chart with some average U.S. household expenditures. It gives you a basic idea of a balanced budget.

CATEGORY	BUDGET PERCENT
Housing (rent/mortgage, utilities and public services, household supplies, furnishings, etc.)	34%
Food (including eating out and to-go food)	13%
Transportation (car, gas, insurance, parking)	18%
Personal care products and services, including clothing and clothing care services	5%
Reading and education	2%
Entertainment (movies, CDs or MP3s, sports events)	5%
Healthcare (dentist, glasses/contacts, HMO)	6%
Personal insurance and retirement plans	11%
Miscellaneous (gifts, vacations, etc.)	2%

3. **Create your own budget.** Use a paper or computer-based spreadsheet to make your own budget based on the sample chart and your own expenses and income. (Your categories and expenses may differ from those in the table.) Estimate the dollar amount for each category. In some categories, you will have greater control than in others. For example, you can limit the number of movies and concerts you go to. But you can't tell the electric company how much you'll pay. Remember that some bills may come only once or twice a year (such as auto insurance). Each month you'll have to put some money aside so you can pay such bills when they're due.

4. **Keep track of what you spend.** Each time you pay for something, enter it in the correct category. At the end of the month, add up what you spent in each area. Keep track of monthly totals.

5. **Learn how to adjust your budget to fit your needs.** Compare your spending to the amounts you have budgeted. Suppose you're spending too much in one area. *You have two choices: Either adjust your budget or spend less.* If you spend too much in one category, you have to decrease that amount in another category.

■ **Thinking It Over:** Write **T** for *true* or **F** for *false*.

1. ____ Following a budget is a good way to control spending.

2. ____ You should never spend more than 2 percent of your income on a vacation.

3. ____ A good guideline for housing and related expenses is 34 percent of your income.

4. ____ Say your rent gets raised. It now makes your housing expenses more than 34 percent of your income. You have no choice but to move.

■ **Everyday Math**

1. The budget chart does not account for 100 percent of income. What percentage is not accounted for? _____

2. Michelle takes home $1,058 a month from her part-time job. She wants to spend 25 of that percent on rent. How much can she afford for rent? $_____

   She has two roommates who will pay the same dollar amount. Together, how much can they afford in rent? $_____

■ **Key Vocabulary**

1. A *budget* is
   _____
   _____.

2. Your *income* is
   _____
   _____.

3. If you can *afford* something, you
   _____
   _____.

4. If you *adjust* something, you
   _____.

5. If you *increase* an amount, you
   _____.

6. If you *decrease* an amount, you
   _____.

■ **Extend the Lesson**

Suppose you want an apartment that will raise your total housing costs to 38 percent of your income. Look at the budget chart. What adjustments could you make so you could take the apartment?

_____
_____
_____
_____

■ **On Your Own**

Name four common budget items that are not listed in the chart on page 12.

_____
_____
_____
_____

UNIT

[1]   REVIEW | Readiness for Independence

A. Recalling What You've Learned

1. Name one general skill and one specific skill that would help you succeed on your own.

   _____   _____

2. Name one negative attitude that can limit your success. Tell how it can hurt you.

   _____

   _____

3. Describe two ways you can keep track of a busy schedule.

   _____   _____

4. How can you determine if you have enough income to live on your own?

   _____

B. What Is It?

1. _____: your basic beliefs, viewpoints, and feelings about life

2. _____: a tool you use to schedule your appointments, dates, and work hours

3. _____: a general guideline for spending your monthly income

C. Achieving Independence

1. Name one negative attitude you have that holds you back. Explain what you can do to change this attitude and the behaviors it causes.

   _____

   _____

   _____

2. Imagine yourself two years from now. What goals toward a more independent life do you hope to have achieved by then?

   _____

   _____

   _____

UNIT
[2]

PREVIEW | Finding an Apartment

■ How much do you already know about the material in this unit? Circle words or letters to correctly complete the sentences. Answers are upside down at the bottom of the page.

1. A one-room apartment is sometimes called a (condo / studio).

2. A renter usually has to pay a deposit (before / after) moving in.

3. The (landlord / manager) is the owner of the rental property.

4. Apartment hunters should check the classified ads (on the bulletin board / in the newspaper or online).

5. On a rental application, you will be asked to list your (income / interests).

6. Roommates tend to get along better if they share the same (life cycle / lifestyle).

7. Abbreviations are used in classified rental ads to save
   a. time.
   b. space.
   c. energy.

8. Living a long way from work would increase your
   a. transportation costs.
   b. travel time.
   c. travel time and transportation costs.

9. The abbreviation *BA* in a classified ad means
   a. bathroom.
   b. back alley.
   c. before applying.

10. As a percentage of income, the cost of housing and related expenses should be no more than
   a. 30–35 percent.
   b. 5–10 percent.
   c. 55–60 percent.

LESSON

1   A Housing Checklist

Griffin and Gia are excited. The 20-year-old twins are ready to move out on their own! They have decided to look for a place to live together. Both have good daytime jobs at the same department store in the local mall. At night, they attend classes at the nearby community college. They've worked hard on their budget. By sharing expenses and pinching pennies, they figure they can afford a monthly rent of $900.

The twins have never shopped for housing before. When they visit an apartment, what features should they look for? What questions should they ask the apartment manager? And how will they compare the pros and cons of different places? After brainstorming, they make a list of their wants and needs. Tomorrow, they're going out looking for vacancy signs. For each apartment they visit, Griffin and Gia will fill out a checklist like the one below.

CHECKLIST

STREET ADDRESS: _____

COST: monthly rent _____   deposits required _____

LOCATION: Safe neighborhood? _____   Noisy street? _____

     Grocery store nearby? _____   Bus stop nearby? _____

     How far from work? _____   How far from school? _____

APARTMENT FEATURES: Clean? _____   Tub in bathroom? _____

     Adequate closet space? _____   Garage or carport? _____

     Major appliances? _____   Air conditioner? _____

     Swimming pool? _____   Workout room? _____

     Laundry facilities? _____   Patio or balcony? _____

     Additional storage provided? _____   Pets allowed? _____

■ Thinking It Over

1. A grocery store near your home is an important

   a. money saver.

   b. safety feature.

   c. convenience

2. A very light sleeper might not want to live

   a. in a hot climate.

   b. on a noisy street.

   c. near the bus stop.

3. The term *laundry facilities* means

   a. soap and dryer.

   b. washer and dryer.

   c. sheets and towels.

4. The term *major appliances* means

   a. stove and refrigerator.

   b. iron and hair dryer.

   c. gas and electricity.

5. A patio or balcony is necessary if you plan to

   a. watch the sun rise.

   b. breathe fresh air.

   c. cook outdoors.

■ Everyday Math

How much money has each twin budgeted for monthly rent?

_____

■ Key Vocabulary

1. Arguments *for* and *against* something are called *p*_____ and *c*_____.

2. An apartment that's available for rent is called a *u*_____

3. *B*_____ means "thinking hard to come up with ideas."

4. A *b*_____ is a plan for spending and saving.

■ Informal Language

What two-word phrase in the reading means "being very careful with even the smallest expenses"?

_____

■ On Your Own

1. What features would *you* look for if you were shopping for housing? Write two items that could be added to the twins' checklist.

   _____

   _____

2. List two or more checklist items that are "wants" rather than "needs."

   _____

   _____

LESSON

2   Comparing Classified Rental Ads

Dante is looking for an apartment. Here are some of the classified ads he recently found online.

Ad 1

> Charming studio apt, w/w, all elec kit, $650, first and last + $325 sec dep. 555-6329 after 5:00.

Ad 3

> 2 BR, 2 BA condo, hardwood floors, AC, w/d in unit, pool, avail Aug. 1, $950 + $600 sec dep. Call Jerry 555-3082

Ad 2

> Furn 1 BR, 1 BA apt., w/w, 1-year lease, $700 first and last + $500 sec dep. Quiet bldg nr river. Avail now. 555-4199.

Ad 4

> Efficiency apt sublease June-Sept. w/w, w/d in bldg, pool, exercise room, $500 + $200 sec dep, util inc. Sherry 555-8972

To understand these ads, Dante must be able to interpret these abbreviations and know the meaning of these words:

ABBREVIATIONS USED IN APARTMENT ADS	WORDS TO KNOW
AC – air conditioner	**condo** – condominium (an apartment unit owned by an individual)
appl – appliances (such as a stove and refrigerator)	**deposit** – money a renter pays to a landlord before moving into an apartment. A deposit pays for any damage renters may do. It is returned if the apartment is left undamaged and clean.
apt – apartment	
avail – available (date the apartment will be ready to rent)	
BA – bathroom	
bldg – building	**efficiency apartment** – a furnished, one-room apartment
BR – bedroom	
elec – electricity, electrical	**first and last** – first and last months' rent
furn – furnished	
incl – includes	**lease** – a written agreement between a landlord and a renter
kit – kitchen	
LR – living room	**studio apartment** – an apartment with one large room and a private bathroom
nr – near	
sec dep – security deposit	
unfurn – unfurnished	**sublease** – to take on the responsibilities of someone else's lease
w/w – wall-to-wall carpeting	
w/d – washer and dryer	

- **Thinking It Over:** Write **T** for *true* or **F** for *false*.

    1. ____ If Dante takes either apartment 3 or 4, he won't have to buy furniture.

    2. ____ If Dante had a roommate who paid half, his best buy would be No. 2.

    3. ____ If Dante takes apartment 1, he'll be able to do his laundry at home.

    4. ____ Dante needs a place just for the summer. His best choice would be apartment 3.

    5. ____ Dante likes to cook with gas. He should avoid apartment 1.

    6. ____ Dante's allergies get worse in carpeted places. The best apartment for him is No. 3.

- **Abbreviations:** Draw a line to connect the abbreviation with its meaning.

1. LR	a.	includes
2. w/w	b.	bedroom
3. sec dep	c.	available
4. BR	d.	living room
5. incl	e.	security deposit
6. avail	f.	wall-to-wall carpeting

- **Everyday Math**

    1. If Dante takes apartment 1, how much money will he have to pay before he can move in? $_____

    2. Suppose Dante takes apartment 3. If he splits the costs with a roommate, how much money will each need to pay before moving in? $_____

- **Sequencing:** Number these apartment-hunting steps in order.

    ____ Call landlord for an appointment to see apartment.

    ____ Fill out application to rent apartment.

    ____ Get keys to apartment.

    ____ Look at apartment.

    ____ Read ad online.

    ____ Sign lease and pay deposits for apartment.

- **Key Vocabulary:** Complete the sentences with words from the reading.

    1. If you _____ an apartment, you take on the responsibilities of someone else's lease.

    2. A landlord often requires a renter to pay the _____ and _____ month's rent in advance.

    3. A _____ is a one-room apartment with a private bathroom.

    4. A _____ _____ is a sum of money paid to the landlord to cover any damages that might occur.

- **On Your Own**

    Would you rather have a small apartment all to yourself or a larger one to share with a roommate or two? Why?

    _____

    _____

    _____

    _____

LESSON

3   Rental Application

Imagine you've just found an apartment you really like. The landlord gives you this rental application to fill out.

RENTAL APPLICATION

Property Address _____ Apt. # _____

Monthly Rental $_____ Security Deposit $_____ Proposed Date of Occupancy _____

Name(s) of Applicant(s) _____

Names of Other Occupants _____

Are any of the above under 18? _____   Pets (Y/N) _____ type _____

_____

Present Address _____

    How long? _____ Reason for leaving _____

    Name and address of owner or agent _____

_____

Last Previous Address _____

_____

    How long? _____ Reason for leaving _____

    Name and address of owner or agent _____

_____

Present Employer _____ How long? _____

    Address _____ Phone _____

    Employed as _____ Salary $ _____ per _____

Credit References (1) _____

    Address _____ Phone _____

    (2) _____

    Address _____ Phone _____

Vehicle License Plate # _____ State of Registration _____

    Make _____ Model _____ Year _____ Color _____

IN CASE OF EMERGENCY

Name of Closest Relative _____ Relationship _____

    Address _____ Phone _____

AUTHORIZATION TO VERIFY INFORMATION

I authorize owner/agent to verify the above information, including but not limited to obtaining a credit report.

Applicant _____ Phone _____ Date _____

Note: If you give a deposit, do so with a check rather than cash. You should always get a receipt, too, which will specify what the deposit is for. Check your state codes, such as California State Civil Code Section 1950.5, which covers deposits and their uses. It also is wise to get a name and phone number for any landlord that you leave paperwork and/or a deposit with. Beware of potential landlords who will not give you any of the above information and a receipt. Also, before you move in, do a walk through to check the condition of the rental, noting or taking pictures of any damages. This list should be referred to when you move out.

■ Thinking It Over

On a rental application . . .

1. What does "proposed date of occupancy" mean? _____
_____

2. Why are you asked to identify the owner of your present apartment? _____
_____

3. Why are you asked to give the reason for leaving your previous address? _____
_____

4. Why does the new landlord want to know who your employer is?
_____
_____

5. Why does the new landlord want to know how much money you make? _____
_____

6. Why are you asked to give two credit references?
_____
_____

7. Give one reason the new landlord might want to know about your car.
_____
_____

■ Everyday Math

Kate's take-home pay is $450 per week. If she counts each month as 4.3 weeks, what is her monthly income? $_____

About how much can she afford to spend on rent? $_____

■ Key Vocabulary: Circle the word or phrase that best completes each sentence.

1. An *occupant* of an apartment is someone who (collects rent / lives there).

2. Your *previous* address is one that you (had before / will have in the future).

3. An *employer* is someone who (pays someone to do a job / works at a job).

4. An *emergency* is a (planned activity for a large group / sudden situation that needs immediate attention).

5. If you give *authorization* to do something, you say someone (can / cannot) do it.

6. To *verify* something means to (pay for it / prove it is true).

■ Drawing Conclusions

The paragraph following the application advises that you get a receipt for a deposit. It also says that the receipt should say what the deposit is for. What is the reason for this advice?
_____
_____

■ On Your Own

On another piece of paper, write a list of credit references and personal references for yourself. (Credit references are companies or individuals who can say that you pay your bills. Personal references are people who can say you would make a good tenant.) Include addresses and phone numbers.

LESSON

4   Rules for Roommates

Having your own place has some definite advantages. If you live alone, you can decorate your place as you like, and you won't have to put up with the petty annoyances that roommates sometimes cause.

But it's quite expensive to have your own place. If you're just starting a new job, you'll save money by sharing expenses. And a roommate is instant company who can introduce you to his or her friends. That automatically increases the number of people in your social circle.

Of course, there are also some negatives to having a roommate. For one thing, you'll lose a certain amount of your privacy. To prevent big

problems with the roommate experience, the two of you might consider drawing up a list of rules.

Here are some rules one pair of roommates put together. Put a check mark by the rules that seem most important to you.

_____ Pay your share of the rent five days before the first of the month.

_____ Pay your share of the utilities and phone bills a week before the due date.

_____ Buy your own groceries.

_____ Keep food and beverages in your own area of refrigerator.

_____ Keep staples on your own shelf in cabinet.

_____ Put your own dishes in dishwasher after each meal or snack.

_____ Clean up stove and counter after cooking.

_____ Keep common areas neat.

_____ Wipe down shower walls and doors after each shower.

_____ Maximum stay for overnight guests is three nights a week.

_____ Do fair share of chores. See list posted on refrigerator.

_____ No loud noise after 10:30 P.M.

_____ No loud noise before 7:00 A.M.

_____ No smoking allowed in apartment.

_____ The person who has the master suite pays 60 percent of the rent.

_____ Occupancy of master suite will change every six months.

- **Thinking It Over:** Write **T** for *true* or **F** for *false*.

1. ____ Living with a roommate is always better than living alone.

2. ____ A roommate can introduce you to his or her circle of friends.

3. ____ A set of rules can make it easier for roommates to get along.

4. ____ Roommates should never be allowed to have overnight guests.

5. ____ Roommates should always split bills equally.

- **Key Vocabulary:** Circle the word or phrase that best completes each sentence.

1. If you *decorate* an apartment, you (make it more attractive / make it neat and tidy).

2. A *petty annoyance* is a (major / minor) disturbance.

3. *Staples* are foods that (you use often / cost a lot).

4. *Financially* means "having to do with (money / finals)."

5. If something happens *automatically*, it happens (just once / without any special effort).

6. The living room and bathroom are (*public / common*) areas.

- **Everyday Math**

1. The rent is $1,250. Max has the master suite, so he pays 60 percent of the rent. How much does he pay each month? $_____

2. No loud noise is allowed between 10:30 P.M. and 7:00 A.M. How many hours is that?   _____

3. Three friends rent a three-bedroom apartment. They decide to split the $1,455 rent equally. How much will each roommate pay? $_____

- **Cause and Effect**

What do you think would happen if one roommate ate the other roommate's groceries without replacing them?

_____

_____

_____

- **On Your Own**

Write two more "rules for roommates" that you think would be important.

_____

_____

_____

_____

_____

UNIT [2]   REVIEW | Finding an Apartment

A. Recalling What You've Learned

1. Name two items you might put on a checklist when you're looking for an apartment.

   _____

2. What's the difference between an *apartment* and a *condo*?

   _____

3. Why does a landlord need to know how much money you make?

   _____

4. Name two advantages to having a roommate.

   _____

B. What Is It?

1. _____: a one-room, furnished apartment

2. _____: money you give a landlord before you move in, to cover possible damages to the apartment

3. _____: one of the two major appliances usually found in an apartment

C. You and Your Apartment

1. Name one quality you would want to see in a potential roommate. Explain why this quality is important to you.

   _____

2. Name one reason a potential roommate might *not* want to live with you. What can you do to change this behavior in yourself?

   _____

   _____

D. What Should You Do?

Your roommate wants to invite a friend to stay at the apartment for the summer. You like the friend and don't mind the extra company. However, you know that the utility and food bills will go up. You can't afford more than you're paying now. What should you do?

_____

_____

PREVIEW | Moving in and Getting Settled

UNIT [3]

■ How much do you already know about the material in this unit? Circle words or letters to correctly complete the sentences. Answers are upside down at the bottom of the page.

1. To let your credit card company know you're moving, send them a (friendly letter / change of address card or form).

2. Once you inform the post office of your new address, your mail will be (returned / forwarded).

3. You should order utilities services (before / after) moving into a new place.

4. The landlord usually pays for (electricity / water).

5. The first time you get a phone in your own name, you'll have to pay a (deposit / penalty).

6. One example of basic furniture is a (CD or MP3 player / bed).

7. To buy towels and sheets, you would go to the _____ section of the store.
   a. linens
   b. appliances
   c. women's wear

8. You can probably find the cheapest prices on basic furniture
   a. at a specialty store.
   b. in online or newspaper classified ads.
   c. at department stores.

9. To get the best price on a moving truck, you should
   a. tell the company what your budget is.
   b. call six weeks in advance.
   c. compare prices of different companies.

10. To reserve a moving truck, you must
    a. pay a deposit.
    b. show your birth certificate.
    c. pay the full bill.

Answers: 1. change of address card/form 2. forwarded 3. before 4. water 5. deposit 6. bed 7. a 8. b 9. c 10. a

LESSON

1   Change of Address Forms

The change of address form put out by the U.S. Postal Service is now almost always done online. The postal service is now encouraging those who can to change their address online at http://www.usps.com/umove. Simply follow the online instructions. You may also use Form 3575 or submit a change of address via telephone.

1. **Who's moving?**

- If it's just you, click the INDIVIDUAL box.

- If it's **some** members of your family with the same last name and others are staying, fill out a **separate form for each mover and click the INDIVIDUAL box.**

- If some members of your family with different last names and others are staying, fill out a **separate form for each mover and click the INDIVIDUAL box.**

- If it's **everyone** in your family with the same last name, just fill out **one** form and click the ENTIRE FAMILY box.

- If it's your business, click the BUSINESS box.

2. **Old address**

Type your **complete** OLD ADDRESS, including an APARTMENT NUMBER, P.O. BOX, or SUITE NUMBER. The abbreviation "RR/HCR No." stands for Rural Route/ Highway Contract Route Number. If this applies to your old address, give us your RR/HCR No. as well as your Box Number.

UNITED STATES POSTAL SERVICE®

Official Change of Address Instructions

It's fast.
It's easy.
It's secure.

Visit usps.com

1 Enter your name and mail forwarding start date.

2 Enter your old and new addresses.*

3 Verify your identity with your personal debit or credit card for fraud protection.

4 Receive immediate email confirmation.

*The following exceptions apply: The U.S. Postal Service® does not forward mail **from** U.S. Military Bases, colleges, universities or from business addresses to residential addresses. Please check with the Military Base, college, university or business for mail forwarding instructions.

IMC-0510

- **Thinking It Over:** Circle the word or phrase that best completes each sentence.

1. The post office is encouraging people to change their address (online / via telephone).

2. Suppose some family members with the same last name are *not* moving. Each person moving (can be listed on the same form / must fill out a separate form).

3. Suppose some members of the same family have *different* last names. Each person moving (must fill out a separate form / can be listed on the same form).

4. If your company is moving, you should check the (Individual / Business) box.

5. Suppose you have three small businesses operating out of your home. You're moving all of them to an office. You will need (one / three) change of address forms.

- **Synonyms and Antonyms:** Write **S** for *synonyms (words with the same meanings)* or **A** for *antonyms (words with opposite meanings)* next to each word pair.

1. ____ moving / staying

2. ____ same / identical

3. ____ separate / distinct

4. ____ entire / part

5. ____ complete / total

6. What word in the lesson is a synonym of *one*?

_____

7. What word in the lesson is an antonym of *permanent*?

_____

- **Everyday Math**

Dylan filled out a change of address form on July 4. He was planning to move on August 15. How many days in advance did he fill out the form? _____ days

How many weeks is that? _____ weeks

- **Drawing Conclusions**

Marion moved in the middle of the school semester. She filled out a change of address form for the post office online. But she forgot to tell the school about her move. What happened when the school mailed her report card?

_____

_____

_____

- **On Your Own**

Make a list of people and companies you would notify if you were about to move.

_____

_____

_____

Ordering Phone, Utilities, and Internet Services

Chris had been packing boxes for a week. He'd carefully wrapped all of his fragile objects. He used enough paper to ensure that they wouldn't get broken in the move. He'd thrown out or given away all the things he'd never use again.

He asked a few friends to help him carry the boxes and furniture onto the van he'd rented. They also said they'd help him carry the boxes off the van and into the new apartment.

Chris was excited about moving out on his own. But about a week before the move, his friend Jesse began asking Chris some questions.

"Did you arrange to get your phone hooked up?" asked Jesse. "Did you call the gas company? What about the electric company? What about water service—is the landlord taking care of that? Do you need to set up an Internet connection?"

Chris hadn't even thought of those details. Jesse handed him a list of things to do. He had found it in a "Mover's Guide" he saw online. Here's what the list said:

IMPORTANT UTILITY INFORMATION

- If you have a landline, call your local phone company for a new number or change of location at least a week before you move. Have service turned off at your old address.

- If you have one, call your long-distance company to ensure uninterrupted service for your long-distance calling plans and other services.

- Have gas, electric, and water service connected the day before you move in. Have these services turned off at your old address the day after you move out.

- Arrange for cable TV and Internet installation at your new address. Check with your cable provider; it may also offer inexpensive phone service with free long distance.

Chris was grateful for the reminder and for the directions. Of course, he wouldn't have the utilities turned off at his old address. His parents and siblings were still living there! Also, he wouldn't need to do anything about the water service. The landlord at the apartment would pay it, along with the trash and recycling bill.

Chris wasn't in a hurry to get a long-distance phone service set up, either. That's because he planned to use his cell phone for long-distance calls. But he also makes a lot of local calls. So he decided that he would get a local phone service. He was eager to get his computer hooked up to the Internet as soon as possible.

■ **Thinking It Over**

1. Name two things Chris did to get ready for his move.

   _____

   _____

2. Name three details Chris had almost forgotten.

   _____

   _____

   _____

■ **Inference:** Write an answer to each question.

1. Why should you call the phone company at least a week before your move?

   _____

   _____

2. Why would you want the gas, electricity, and water turned on the day *before* you move in? Wouldn't it be better to wait until the day you get there?

   _____

   _____

   _____

3. Why would you want the gas, electricity, and water turned off the day *after* you move out? Wouldn't it be better to have it done the same day as your move?

   _____

   _____

   _____

   _____

■ **Key Vocabulary:** Complete the sentences with words from the reading. Use first letters as clues.

1. Wrapping delicate glass in paper helps to *e*_____ that it won't break during the move.

2. You should call the utility companies to *a*_____ for service.

3. The *d*_____ of a move are all the little things you need to remember.

4. If service is *u*_____, you won't be without it for even a day.

5. If you are *g*_____ for something, you are thankful for it.

6. Someone who gives you a *r*_____ makes sure you don't forget.

7. Another word for *brothers and sisters* is *s*_____.

■ **On Your Own**

When you order phone service, you're sometimes asked if you want certain extras. For example, you might be offered call waiting, caller identification, or voicemail services. How important are these services to you? Do you think they are worth the extra money?

   _____

   _____

LESSON

3   Buying Essential Household Goods

FURNITURE

If you're just starting out, you probably won't have much furniture of your own. Even if you own some large pieces, you might decide not to move them. After all, it can be very expensive to move furniture—especially if you're moving far away. Sometimes you're better off selling your old stuff and buying new or used furniture in your new city.

    Here are some smart options for acquiring furniture.

Check with your relatives. Family members are often glad to help young people get started. Perhaps your grandparents have an old sofa they don't need anymore. Or maybe an uncle or aunt has recently bought new bedroom furniture and can pass along their old pieces. So, get the word out that you're moving into your own place soon. You might be surprised by the help you'll be offered!

Renting or leasing furniture. If you're not sure how long you'll stay in your new home, this is a good option. Usually, you'll have to sign a one-year lease. If you rent for a shorter period, your monthly price will be higher. What is the advantage of renting or leasing furniture? You can fill up an entire apartment for relatively little money. But the disadvantage, of course, is that, even after a year of payments, you won't own anything.

Buying furniture. You can buy new or used furniture in all price ranges. Check the Salvation Army, Goodwill, and St. Vincent de Paul stores for decent used furniture. Also check out private secondhand stores, garage and yard sales, auctions, and thrift shops. Another possibility is to look at the classified ads in the newspaper or online.

    If you want new furniture, compare prices at discount furniture and department stores.

Making furniture. You'd be surprised how easy it is to make some kinds of furniture. Coffee tables, end tables, desks, lamps, bookcases, a bed—and even a sofa—can be made with a few basic materials and tools. Many books are available that show you how to do this.

OTHER BASIC SUPPLIES

In addition to furniture, you'll need some kitchen utensils and dishes. You'll also need bathroom supplies, linens (sheets and towels), and small appliances such as a clock radio, an iron, a vacuum cleaner, a toaster, and a coffee maker. As with furniture, it's a good idea to compare prices carefully before you buy anything. You can find good buys in many discount stores.

■ **Thinking It Over:** Write **T** for *true* or **F** for *false*.

1. ____ The farther away you move, the more expensive it is to move your furniture.

2. ____ You will probably have to sign a one-year contract to lease furniture.

3. ____ A three-month furniture rental will cost less per month than a 12-month lease.

4. ____ You can buy new furniture at discount and department stores.

5. ____ The prices at discount stores are always cheaper than department stores.

■ **Everyday Math**

1. Macy knows that she will only stay in her one-bedroom apartment for a year, so she doesn't want to buy furniture. Instead, she will spend $150 a month to lease enough furniture for the apartment. How much will she spend in a year? $_____

2. At a used furniture store, Sean paid $210 for a sofa, $65 for an upholstered chair, and $150 for a kitchen table with four chairs. How much did he spend in all? $_____

■ **Key Vocabulary:** Circle the word that best completes the sentence.

1. If something is *essential*, it is (needed / extra).

2. Another word for *acquiring* is (giving / getting).

3. If you do something for the sake of *convenience*, you do it because it is (easier / harder).

4. An *advantage* is something that (is / is not) in your favor.

5. If you *lease* something, you usually rent it for one (month / year).

■ **Making Inferences:** Circle the letter of the correct answer.

1. If you put legs on a door and covered it with a cloth, you'd have a
   a. sofa.
   b. coffee table.
   c. bookcase.

2. If you put legs on a door and placed a foam mattress on top, you'd have a
   a. guest bed.
   b. nightstand.
   c. desk.

3. If you laid a door over two short filing cabinets, you'd have a
   a. bookcase.
   b. dining table.
   c. desk.

■ **On Your Own**

Describe the living room you'd like to have in your first home. Mention the colors, the type of furniture (antique? contemporary?), and other details.

_____

_____

_____

_____

LESSON

4 Renting a Moving Truck

You're very lucky if you're working for a big company that pays for your move. In that case, you can hire movers who will even pack your boxes for you! But if you're like most people, you'll have to pay for your own move. So, you'll probably have to rent a moving truck or a trailer.

If you have only a few boxes and pieces of furniture, a trailer might be big enough. If so, make sure the trailer hitch will fit on the back of the car that you plan to use. Also, be sure the car has enough horsepower to pull a trailer without being damaged. The rental company will be able to provide you with this information.

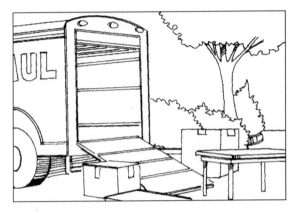

If you need to rent a moving truck, here are a few things you should know:

- How is renting a truck like renting a car? You have many options.

- Some companies charge a flat fee, and you pay for gas.

- Other companies charge mileage, a fee, and refund your gas expenses.

- The rental agency will need to know that you are of legal age. You cannot rent a truck if you are under 18.

- Before you sign a rental contract, you will have to show a valid driver's license.

- You will need insurance on the rental truck. Perhaps you'll be covered by your own personal auto insurance. Some policies cover you in any rental, including a rental truck. If so, you won't have to buy more insurance from the rental company. Check with your insurance company to see if you're already covered.

- Most truck rental businesses have their equipment reserved several weeks in advance. Be sure to call for a reservation early. If you wait too long, you might not be able to get a truck.

- The size of the truck determines the price. Don't rent a bigger truck than you need. For a one-bedroom apartment, a 14-foot van should be enough. For a two-bedroom apartment, you'll probably need a 17-foot van.

■ Thinking It Over

1. Suppose you have only a few boxes, a bed, and a nightstand to move. You'll probably need to rent a (truck / trailer).

2. Imagine that you have enough furniture to fill a two-bedroom apartment. You will need to rent a (14-foot van / 17-foot van).

3. If you rent a trailer, make sure your car is (strong enough / new enough) to pull it.

4. It's a good idea to reserve a moving truck a few (days / weeks) in advance.

■ Everyday Math

Darryl rents a truck for $49.95 a day. He keeps it for 2 days and drives it 120 miles in all. The mileage charge is 40 cents per mile. The gas costs him $36. How much does Darryl have to pay, not counting tax? $_____

■ Key Vocabulary

1. If you *hire* movers, you (help them out /pay them to help you).

2. Another word for *options* is (opinions / choices).

3. If you pay a *flat fee* for a rental truck, you (do / do not) have to pay extra for each mile you drive.

4. The term *legal age* means (16 or 17 / 18 or 21), depending on the state where you live.

5. A valid driver's license (is recognized by the law / proves the person is 21).

■ Giving Advice

Suppose your friend is moving to another state. He wants to move everything he owns, including all his clothing, books, posters, and magazines. What advice would you give him?

_____

_____

_____

_____

■ On Your Own

Make a list of items you'd want to get rid of before moving to a new place.

_____

_____

_____

_____

_____

_____

_____

UNIT [3]

REVIEW | Moving in and Getting Settled

A. Recalling What You've Learned

1. Suppose you're moving in two weeks. In addition to the post office, name two places you'd send a change of address form or card to.

   _____   _____

2. When should you have old utilities turned off and new ones turned on? Explain the reasons for this.

   _____

   _____

3. Explain three ways you can get furniture at reasonable prices.

   _____

   _____

4. What are some costs that may be involved in renting a moving truck?

   _____

B. What Is It?

1. _____: the utility service that enables you to have lights and to turn on your TV

2. _____: the utility service you need if you want to be connected to the Internet

3. _____: three examples of essential household goods

C. Moving and You

Think about the personal items you now own. Which of these things would make you feel more "at home" in a new place? Which could you get rid of and not miss very much? _____

_____

_____

D. What Should You Do?

Your roommate has a couch you don't like very much. She doesn't like it, either, but she says it's better than nothing at all. What options do you have?

_____

_____

PREVIEW | Solving Common Problems

■ How much do you already know about the material in this unit? Circle words or letters to correctly complete the sentences. Answers are upside down at the bottom of the page.

1. Suppose your apartment building has a laundry room on each floor. Your clothes have gone though the dryer cycle. You're expected to (leave them in the dryer / remove them promptly).

2. You want to paint the walls purple in your rented apartment. You should (first ask the landlord / go ahead and do it).

3. You have to replace a broken window at your own expense. As yet, your tight budget has not allowed for this. You will have to (reduce spending in another budget area / live with a broken window for a while).

4. An example of an unexpected expense might be (dental work / your cable bill).

5. One roommate eats two meals a day at the school cafeteria. The other roommate eats all meals at home. The best system for them would be to
   a. split grocery bills evenly.
   b. buy their own groceries.
   c. eat out more often.

6. A renter has moved into an apartment. Now, it is the ___ responsibility to keep it clean.
   a. manager's
   b. landlord's
   c. renter's

7. The water heater in your rented apartment has broken. The ___ must pay to get it fixed.
   a. landlord
   b. renter
   c. plumber

8. The landlord is selling the condo you've been renting. You're required to let him in to show it
   a. if he gives you 7 days notice.
   b. whenever he knocks on the door.
   c. if he gives you 24 hours notice.

Answers: 1. remove them promptly 2. first ask the landlord 3. reduce spending in another budget area 4. dental work 5. b 6. c 7. a 8. c

LESSON

1 Dos and Don'ts for Tenants

Kenji has just moved. He's rented a condo on the second floor of a large building. It has a nice deck overlooking the pool area. It also has a fairly spacious storage area right off the deck. Kenji has a one-year lease, and he is looking forward to settling in. Here is what he plans to do as soon as he gets unpacked:

• Plant tomatoes and flowering vines in pots and put them on the deck. He will train the vines to grow around the deck railing and up the walls on the sides of the deck.

• Install a surround-sound system so he can really enjoy his music and the TV. He'll put some speakers outside on the deck, too.

• Get a large hamper with a cloth bag liner. This way, he can carry all of his laundry to the laundry room at once. He plans to leave it there until all his laundry loads are done. Because the dryers are so expensive, he will dry towels outside on the deck.

• Buy a cord of wood and store it on the deck. It will be handy there, and he won't have to keep buying wood for the fireplace.

• Paint the bedroom walls red and get a black bedspread.

Here is part of the agreement Kenji signed with the owner of the condo. Read it once. Then, look back at Kenji's list. Cross out the things he won't *be able to do.*

■ All exterior areas that are open to public view must be kept neat. Nothing shall be stored on the tiled area outside individual front doors. Items allowed on decks are limited to patio furniture and potted plants. Residents shall not allow climbing or clinging plants to grow up the walls of the buildings or on deck railings. Except for ground floor units, no planter or other container may be set on the railing of a deck. All planters, inside and out, must have a water reservoir to stop water runoff.

■ No exterior clotheslines shall be installed or maintained. There shall be no outside drying of clothes, carpets, or the like, on any unit or the common area. Laundry rooms are to be kept free of litter. Clothes must be removed promptly from machines.

■ No loud music or other noises that could disturb other tenants is permitted.

■ Any permanent improvement to the interior must be approved by the owner in advance. This includes painting and wallpapering.

36

■ Thinking It Over

1. The most likely reason the owner doesn't want vines growing on walls is that

   a. she doesn't like vines.

   b. they can damage the outer walls.

   c. watering them is too expensive.

2. The surround-sound system *inside* the condo will be acceptable as long as Kenji

   a. keeps the sound at a reasonable level.

   b. leaves it behind when he moves.

   c. never uses it.

3. Kenji should probably not install *outside* speakers because

   a. they will get damaged by the elements.

   b. birds might build nests on them.

   c. the sound will disturb his neighbors.

4. If Kenji wants to buy a large supply of wood, he should store it

   a. at the lumber yard.

   b. in his storage area.

   c. at his parents' house.

5. The reason tenants must remove their laundry promptly is that

   a. someone else might want to use the washer or dryer.

   b. laundry left in the machines begins to smell bad.

   c. the machines can cause damage to the clothes.

■ Everyday Math

Kenji plants tomato seedlings in some pots on May 15. The packaging says he will have tomatoes in about 8 weeks. On what date can Kenji expect to pick his first tomatoes? _____

_____

■ Key Vocabulary: Write **S** if the word pairs are *synonyms* (same meaning) or **A** if they are *antonyms* (opposite meanings).

1. _____ spacious / crowded

2. _____ exterior / interior

3. _____ reservoir / holder

4. _____ promptly / quickly

5. _____ permitted / forbidden

■ Making Inferences

1. Why is it against the rules for upper-story residents to put potted plants on deck railings?

   _____

   _____

2. Why does the owner care if the tenant paints the walls or installs wallpaper? _____

   _____

   _____

■ On Your Own

Would you rather live in a spacious, modern condo with a deck or in a smaller, older house with a yard? Why?

_____

_____

_____

LESSON 2

Unexpected Expenses—Revising Your Budget

Have you ever heard the expression, "Expect the unexpected"? This is certainly good advice when it comes to your budget. Suppose you make a budget and it looks as if it will work. You go along for six months, and you have enough money to cover all your expenses. Then an unexpected problem comes along. Maybe something major goes wrong with your car. Maybe your dentist says you need some root canal work. Perhaps your computer crashes. Whatever it is, you haven't planned for it. Suppose you're determined not to touch your savings. What can you do?

Here's a sample budget for someone whose income is $2,000 a month. Circle the *variable* expenses—that is, the costs that can change from month to month.

MONTHLY BUDGET

Rent – $500

Utilities (gas, electricity, water, garbage) – $100

Phone – $55

Cable TV and Internet – $80

Savings – $100

Insurance (health, renter's, car) – $200

Charities – $20

Charge accounts – $120

Medical/dental (drugs and treatment not covered by insurance) – $50

Transportation (car payment, gas, oil, parking) – $300

Household maintenance (cleaning products, repairs) – $30

Food (groceries, nonfood items in supermarket bill, restaurants) – $260

Personal maintenance (clothing, laundry, haircuts, health and grooming products) – $50

Movie subscription service – $15

Recreation – $120

Now, imagine that this person has some car trouble. He needs the car to get to work, so he can't put off fixing it. The repairs will cost $628. He decides to put the charge on a credit card and pay it off within 6 months. Including interest, he figures it will cost him $672, or $112 a month.

Where will he get this $112? He decides to reduce his savings to $75 a month for a while. He thinks he can save another $30 a month by going out to eat less and taking his lunch to work more often. By conserving energy at home, he hopes to save some money on utilities. And he thinks he can trim a few dollars off his recreation spending. Finally, he could reduce his movie subscription service, or even cancel it, for a few months. Right now this is a luxury he can't afford.

You can use the same method when you have unexpected bills. Revising your budget as necessary will help you avoid going deeply in debt. Another option is to purchase renter's insurance. This insurance covers unexpected expenses, such as replacing the contents of your apartment in case of a fire or a break-in. Typically, renter's insurance premiums cost from $150 to $400 a year—an added expense, yes, but less costly than replacing your valuables.

■ **Thinking It Over:** Write **T** for *true* or **F** for *false*.

1. ____ If you stick to a budget, you can avoid unexpected expenses.

2. ____ Some budget items do not change from month to month.

3. ____ The amount you spend on recreation can vary.

4. ____ A movie subscription service should be part of everyone's budget.

5. ____ You can reduce your food expenses by limiting restaurant visits.

6. ____ Your car payment is only part of what it costs to own a car.

■ **Summarizing**

What should you do when you're faced with an unexpected expense? Summarize the points in this lesson.

_____

_____

_____

_____

■ **Everyday Math**

1. A trip to the dentist forces Gloria to face an unexpected bill of $535. Her dentist will let her pay in installments with no interest. If Gloria wants to pay the bill within 4 months, how much will she have to pay each month? $_____

2. Carson accidentally ruined the carpeting in his apartment. Replacing it will cost $950. He has been saving $250 a month. He decides to reduce the amount he saves each month by 50 percent and apply it toward the carpeting. How many months will it take him to pay for the carpeting?   _____

■ **Key Vocabulary:** Write a letter to match each **boldface** word with its meaning.

1. __ **revising**   a. a pleasurable extra

2. __ **advice**   b. saving

3. __ **expenses**   c. way of doing something

4. __ **major**   d. costs

5. __ **sample**   e. lessen

6. __ **reduce**   f. example

7. __ **conserving**   g. words of wisdom

8. __ **luxury**   h. changing

9. __ **method**   i. great in size or amount

■ **On Your Own**

Make a list of some unexpected expenses you've had in the last year.

_____

_____

_____

_____

_____

_____

LESSON

3   Revising Rules for Roommates

When Gina, Leila, and Kym moved in together, they made up a list of rules. Each young woman has her own copy of these rules:

- Pay your share of rent on the first of the month. (If you cause us to have late fees, you have to pay them.)

- Pay your share of utility and phone bills on the 15th of the month.

- Do not eat other people's food without permission.

- Label your staples in cabinets. Use only your own!

- Label your food and beverages and keep them on your own shelf in fridge.

- Wash your own dishes and clean up after yourself in kitchen.

- Store personal belongings in your own room.

- Take turns cleaning the bathroom. Every third day is your turn!

- Conserve energy. Turn off lights you're not using. Don't run water needlessly.

- Secure all common belongings (such as shared bicycles or scooters) in the locked storage area and make sure to close and lock all doors and windows at night or when you leave the apartment.

- No loud music.

- No smoking.

Three months went by with no difficulties. Then the roommates started noticing a problem. The bread each person would buy on Saturday turned stale and moldy before it was half gone. Packages of lunchmeat started to go bad before they were used. When each person bought a bunch of bananas, the bananas were all rotten within three days. They had to throw out milk, eggs, and other foods because they went bad. And they were wasting staples too. Crackers and cereal often got stale soon after being opened. So, the roommates decided to have a meeting and revise their rules.

"Here's my idea," Gina said. "Let's make a food budget and share the cost and the food. That way, we can cut down on the waste. Instead of buying three loaves of bread all at once, we'll buy one and share it. Then we'll buy another one. That way, we won't be throwing out stale bread every few days. Instead of buying three pounds of hamburger, we'll buy one and share it. The same goes for all the food we've been wasting. We can each put the same amount of money into the pot. Then we can take turns shopping, using a list. That makes more sense, don't you think?"

"That will work for us," Kym said, "since we all eat pretty much the same things and the same amounts. Each of us spends about the same amount on food, don't we? So, this new system sounds good. Let's try it and see how it goes."

"Good idea," said Leila. "If it doesn't seem to work, we can always have another meeting. We might have to revise the rules a few times before we nail them down once and for all."

Thinking It Over

1. The roommates agreed that
   a. the person who caused late fees had to pay them.
   b. they would all be vegetarians.
   c. overnight guests were not allowed.

2. Utility and phone bills were to be paid on the
   a. last day of the month.
   b. first day of the month.
   c. 15th day of the month.

3. If Leila cleaned the bathroom on Monday, she had to do it again on
   a. Tuesday.
   b. Thursday.
   c. Saturday.

4. Regarding music, the roommates' rule was
   a. no country music.
   b. no '70s music.
   c. no loud music.

Everyday Math

1. Based on the new plan for grocery shopping, the budget was $75 a week. How much would each roommate have to pay? $_____ a week

2. How much was the total grocery budget for 3 months (13 weeks)? $_____

Key Vocabulary: Circle the word that best completes each sentence.

1. If you are *invited* to do something, you are (asked / told) to do it.

2. When you *conserve* energy, you (waste / save) it.

3. If you do something *needlessly*, you do it for (no / a good) reason.

4. *Noticing* something means (missing / seeing) it.

5. If something is *stale*, it is (fresh / old).

Idioms

1. "Putting money into the pot" means that everyone (contributes / takes) something.

2. *Fridge* is a short form of the word (freezer / refrigerator).

3. If you "nail something down," you get it (right / wrong).

Cause and Effect

Why is it important for the roommates to secure common belongings and to remember to lock windows and doors at night or when they leave the apartment? What might happen if they didn't?

_____

_____

On Your Own

Look over the list of rules in the reading. Find one rule you think should be revised. Write the revision, and explain why you think the change is an improvement.

_____

_____

_____

_____

_____

LESSON

4   Tenants' Legal Rights

It was February, and the weather was very cold. Casey noticed a serious problem in the apartment he was renting. The heater didn't work. He called his landlord and left a message about the broken heater on the answering machine. By the end of the following day, the landlord had still not returned Casey's call.

So, Casey wrote a letter to the landlord. A week passed. Still he heard nothing. That's when Casey decided to get the heater fixed himself. He would deduct the cost of the repairs from his next rent payment.

Is Casey allowed to do this? The answer is yes. In fact, he could have done it after only a few days because the weather was so cold. Like all tenants, Casey has certain rights.

Read the list of landlords' legal responsibilities in Casey's state. The laws in other states may differ. If you rent an apartment, condo, or house, you should find out about such laws in your own state.

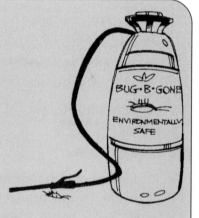

A landlord must:

1. Correct violations of health or housing codes that endanger tenants' health or safety.

2. Keep common areas reasonably clean and safe from defects that could cause fires or other accidents.

3. Provide a smoke detector.

4. Make sure the rental property is not infested with rodents, insects, or other pests when the tenant moves in. Control pests during the tenancy, except in the case of a single-family residence.

5. Keep the rental in as good repair as it was or should have been at the beginning of tenancy. Normal wear and tear is acceptable.

6. Provide adequate locks and keys.

7. Keep electrical, plumbing, and heating systems in good repair. Repair any appliances or other facilities that are supplied for renters' use.

8. Keep the rental unit weathertight.

9. Provide garbage cans. Arrange for trash removal for tenants, except for those who occupy single-family residences.

10. Provide access to a reasonable amount of heat, as well as hot and cold water.

■ **Thinking It Over:** Write **T** for *true* or **F** for *false*.

1. ____ If the built-in microwave oven breaks, the landlord must repair or replace it.

2. ____ A very old building has a cockroach problem. Controlling the roaches in each apartment is the renter's responsibility.

3. ____ When it rains, moisture seeps in through the window frames, even if they are closed. This is a problem the landlord must fix.

4. ____ The tenant's toaster oven broke. The landlord must replace it.

5. ____ In a 24-unit building, most tenants can't get hot water unless they shower very early. The landlord must get bigger water heaters.

■ **Everyday Math**

State law says that tenants can make necessary repairs and deduct the cost from the rent. However, in any 12-month period, the tenant can spend no more than two months' rent total on repairs. Mick's rent is $650. In July, he spent $875 to replace a refrigerator that didn't work. Now, his air conditioner is broken. What is the most he can spend on it? $_____

If the repair job costs more than that, what should Mick do?

_____

_____

■ **Key Vocabulary:** Circle the word or phrase that best completes each sentence.

1. The opposite of *serious* is (important / trivial).

2. If you *deduct* something, you (take it away / add it).

3. If something is *allowed*, it is (forbidden / permitted).

4. *Tenants* are people who (own / rent) an apartment or a house.

5. To *occupy* a place is to (own it / live there).

6. *Adequate* means (enough / plenty).

■ **Cause and Effect**

What do you think would happen if a landlord ignored a leaky roof?

_____

_____

_____

_____

_____

■ **On Your Own**

What would you do if your landlord ignored your requests to have the heater repaired?

_____

_____

_____

UNIT [4] REVIEW | Solving Common Problems

A. Recalling What You've Learned

1. Name two things a tenant in a large apartment complex should avoid doing.

   _____

   _____

2. Explain what you should do when you're faced with an unexpected expense.

   _____

3. Suppose one roommate out of three is always late with the rent. What should the other roommates do about it?

   _____

   _____

4. Name three legal rights that all tenants have.

   _____

   _____

B. What Is It?

1. An example of a tenant's behavior that can disturb other tenants is

   _____

2. A bill that comes as a surprise is an _____

   Give an example. _____

3. One example of a tenant's legal rights is _____

C. Common Problems and You

1. Identify a trait you could never put up with in a roommate. Then explain why this behavior annoys you so much. _____

   _____

2. Suppose you're a landlord. Your tenant has asked if she can have a dog. You're afraid a dog could damage the carpeting. On the other hand, you don't want to lose this good tenant. What will be your answer be? Why? _____

   _____

WORD LIST | Moving Out on Your Own

Abbreviations
access
account
achievement
acquired
actions
address
adequate
adjust
adulthood
advantages
afford
annoyances
apartment
appliances
application
appointments
appropriately
assessment
attitude
authorize
automatically

Balance
balcony
behavior
beverages
brainstorming
budget
bully

Cable TV
cafeteria
calendar
carport
categories
charities
checklist
chore
classified ads
cockroach
codes
competencies
complex
compromise
computer
condominium
confident
conserve
constructive criticism
contemporary
cooperative
credit card
credit references

Debt
decrease
defects
defiant
delicate
dentist
department store
dependence
deposit
details
determine

discount
disturb
dryer
due

Eager
efficient
employer
enables
endanger
energy
ensure
equipment
essential
establish
express
exterior

Facilities
features
financial
flat fee
furnished

Goals
gossips
graphs
groceries
guideline

Hamper
hectic
horsepower
household
housing

Immature
impression

income
increase
independence
infested
insecurity
insurance
interior
Internet
interpret
interview
introduce
inventory

Know-it-all
knowledge

Landlord
late fees
laundry
lease
legal age
lifestyle
limit
linens
litter
local
long-term
luxury

Magazines
maintenance
major
maximum
method
microwave
mileage
model
modern

moisture
moldy

Negative

Occasions
occupants
online
options

Patio
paycheck
peer pressure
penalty
percentage
perfectionist
permanent
permitted
personal
petty
plumber
positive
posted
posture
potential
previous
price ranges
privacy
promptly
proposed

Quality

Readiness
receipt
recreation
relative
reluctant

rent
rental unit
repairs
replace
reserve
reservoir
residence
residents
responsibility
résumé
reveal
revise
rights
rodents
roommates
routine

Salary
schedule
secondhand
self-defeating
semester
siblings
smoke detector
social
sofa
spacious
specific
stale
standard
staples
storage
studio
summarize
surround-sound system

Tardy
task

taxes
tenants
to-do list
trailer
trait

U.S. Postal Service
unexpected
uninterrupted
upper-story
utilities

Vacancy
valid

van
variable
verify
victim
viewpoint
violations
voicemail
vote

Wallpaper
waste
weathertight
withheld